S0-AIM-886

12 JOURNALISTS AND MEDIA PERSONALITIES
WITH DISABILITIES

by Marne Ventura

12

STORY LIBRARY
MORE TO EXPLORE

www.12StoryLibrary.com

Copyright © 2020 by 12-Story Library, Mankato, MN 56002. All rights reserved. No part of this book may be reproduced or utilized in any form or by any means without written permission from the publisher.

12-Story Library is an imprint of Bookstaves.

Photographs ©: Stacey Newman/Shutterstock.com, cover, 1; MSNBC/YouTube, 4; Hadrian/Shutterstock.com, 5; PD, 5-7; Everett Historical/Shutterstock.com, 7; Levan Ramishvili/PD, 8; Levan Ramishvili/PD, 9; PjrNews/Alamy, 10; Leon Mosley/YouTube, 11; Paul fromMN/YouTube, 12; Paul fromMN/YouTube, 13; Kemberly Groue/PD, 13; Cerebral Palsy Foundation/YouTube, 14; Jonathan Newton/The Washington Post/Getty Images, 15; Cerebral Palsy Foundation/YouTube, 15; Featureflash Photo Agency/Shutterstock.com, 16; Getty Images, 17; Mid Western University/YouTube, 18; Madan Puraskar Organization/CC3.0, 19; PD, 19; Anne Davie/YouTube, 20; Gogglebox Girls/YouTube, 21; Stacey Newman/Shutterstock.com, 22; Molly Riley/UPI/Alamy, 23; HuffPost/YouTube, 24; HuffPost/YouTube, 25; David Davies/PA Images/Alamy, 26; Mark Davidson/Alamy, 27; Steve Brown GB/YouTube, 27; AnnGaysorn/Shutterstock.com, 28; Andrey_Popov/Shutterstock.com, 29

ISBN
9781632357557 (hardcover)
9781632358646 (paperback)
9781645820390 (ebook)

Library of Congress Control Number: 2019938640

Printed in the United States of America
October 2019

About the Cover

Anderson Cooper in 2016.

Access free, up-to-date content on this topic plus a full digital version of this book. Scan the QR code on page 31 or use your school's login at 12StoryLibrary.com.

Table of Contents

Serge Kovaleski: Prize Winning Investigative Reporter 4

Laura Redden Searing: Poet and Civil War Reporter 6

Charles Krauthammer: Influential Conservative Voice 8

Gary O'Donoghue: Covering US Politics for the BBC 10

Darcy Pohland: Getting the Story 12

Jason Benetti: Hitting a Home Run 14

Ade Adepitan: Paralympian and TV Presenter 16

Jhamak Ghimire: Nepal's Helen Keller 18

Lucy Martin: Weather Presenter and Role Model 20

Anderson Cooper: Following His Passion 22

Wendy Lu: Activist Journalist 24

Steve Brown: Living His Dream 26

Learn More: Facts and Figures 28

Glossary 30

Read More 31

Index 32

About the Author 32

Serge Kovaleski: Prize-Winning Investigative Reporter

Serge Kovaleski in 2010.

the joints and muscles in one hand short and tight. At Dwight High School in Manhattan, Kovaleski played soccer and started a rock band called Triage. He wrote songs and played bass guitar.

In 1984, Kovaleski graduated from the College of William & Mary in Virginia. Then he traveled in Europe. He became interested in reporting. Back in the United States, he started his career at the *Miami News*. Then he worked as a reporter for the *Washington Post* and the *New York Daily News*.

Serge Kovaleski is an American reporter. He was born in Cape Town, South Africa, in 1961. He grew up in Australia. His family moved to New York in the 1970s. Kovaleski was born with a condition called arthrogryposis. This makes

Kovaleski joined the *New York Times* in 2006. He covered big stories like the Aurora, Colorado, movie theater shooting. Another was the Boston Marathon bombing. In 2018, he wrote about the Las Vegas massacre.

INVESTIGATIVE REPORTING

Kovaleski is an investigative reporter. He looks into public matters where something is hidden or not known to the public. Topics might be crimes, political corruption, or misdeeds by people in power. Investigative reporters are like detectives. They might spend months or even years researching and writing a story.

2009

Year when Serge Kovaleski was part of a team that won a Pulitzer Prize

- Kovaleski and his team reported on a scandal. It involved the governor of New York.
- He was part of the team that reported on the Navy's SEAL Team 6 and their raid on Osama bin Laden.
- Kovaleski has also reported on the arts and music.

2

Laura Redden Searing: Poet and Civil War Reporter

Laura Redden Searing was an American writer. Born in 1839, she grew up in St. Louis, Missouri. At age 11, she became ill with meningitis. It caused her to lose her hearing. At the Missouri School for the Deaf, she learned sign language. She began writing poetry. She performed one of her poems in sign language at graduation.

Searing returned to St. Louis and became a newspaper editor. It was the year before the start of the Civil War. She wrote pro-Union essays for the *St. Louis Republican*. She used the pen name Howard Glyndon. The war began in April 1861. Searing went to Washington, DC, and kept writing for the *Republican*. She reported on the war and politics. She interviewed President Lincoln and General Ulysses S. Grant.

After the war, Searing went to Europe. She studied French, German, Italian and Spanish. She wrote stories for the *New York Times* and the *New York Sun*. Back in the United States, she married Edward Searing. They had a daughter named Elsa.

1872

Year when a city in Minnesota was named Glyndon, after Laura Redden Searing's pen name

- Searing wrote a book of poems about the Civil War. *Idyls of Battle* was published in 1864 under the name Howard Glyndon.
- The book was very popular, and Glyndon received many fan letters.
- The Minnesota city was founded by a Civil War veteran.

SEARING'S PEN NAME

A rival newspaper in the South published a negative article about Searing. Its purpose was to expose her use of a pen name and discredit her. Instead, it made her better known as a journalist. Searing never hid the fact that she was a woman, or that she was deaf.

IDYLS OF BATTLE

AND

POEMS OF THE REBELLION.

BY HOWARD GLYNDON.

(LAURA C. REDDEN.)

Searing published in *Harper's Weekly* under the pen name Howard Glyndon.

Charles Krauthammer: Influential Conservative Voice

Charles Krauthammer was an American journalist. He was born in 1950 in New York City. His parents were Jews who fled Europe at the start of World War II. The family moved to Canada when Krauthammer was five. They spent summers in New York. Krauthammer graduated in 1970 from McGill University in Montreal.

He was editor of the school newspaper.

Krauthammer studied for a year in Oxford University in England. Then he entered Harvard Medical School. While swimming in the campus pool, he jumped from the diving board and hit his head. The impact broke his spinal cord. At age 22, he was paralyzed from the waist down. Krauthammer was in the hospital for 14 months. He kept up his schoolwork. He graduated on schedule in 1975 and became a psychiatrist.

In 1978, he moved to Washington, DC. He became research director at the National Institute of Mental Health (NIMH). He began to write about politics for the *New Republic* magazine. Before long, he left medicine to be a writer. Krauthammer wrote for the *New Republic* from 1981 to 2011. He

Charles Krauthammer in 1985.

Krauthammer in his Washington, DC, office in 2010.

wrote for *Time* magazine from 1983 to 2018. He was a commentator on PBS and Fox News. From 1984 until his death in 2018, he wrote a weekly opinion column for the *Washington Post*.

THINK ABOUT IT

Krauthammer believed in honest debate as a way to get to the truth. How is this important for a democracy?

1987

Year when Charles Krauthammer won the Pulitzer Prize

- In 2006, the *Financial Times* named him the most influential commentator in America.
- He was known for his funny, thoughtful writing.
- Early in his career, Krauthammer's political views changed from liberal to conservative.

Gary O'Donoghue: Covering US Politics for the BBC

and played football. At Oxford University, he studied philosophy and languages.

While in college, O'Donoghue interned at the BBC. He worked in the Braille department. People told him he would never become a

1987
Year when Charles Krauthammer won the Pulitzer Prize

- In 2006, the *Financial Times* named him the most influential commentator in America.
- He was known for his funny, thoughtful writing.
- Early in his career, Krauthammer's political views changed from liberal to conservative.

Gary O'Donoghue is a British journalist. He was born in England in 1969. His father was a football player and taxi driver. His mother was a dance teacher. O'Donoghue's vision was impaired when he was born. By age eight, he had lost all sight. At Worcester College for the Blind, he studied

Gary O'Donoghue reporting live on BBC News in 2017.

BBC NEWS   14:15   MONTH AT THE FASTEST PACE SINCE JUNE 2(

reporter because of his blindness. After graduating, he was hired as a reporter for BBC Radio. He covered stories in Africa, Asia, Europe, and the United States. In 2004, he became a political reporter for radio, TV, and the internet.

In 2007, O'Donoghue found out and wrote about an important piece of breaking news. His editor took him off the story and gave it to another reporter. O'Donoghue sued for discrimination on the grounds of disability. He won the lawsuit.

In 2011, he became chief political correspondent for BBC Radio 4.

In 2014, O'Donoghue moved to Washington, DC, as chief North America political correspondent for BBC News. It's a big, important job. Technology has helped make it a bit easier. When O'Donoghue started out, he had to ask coworkers or friends to read information to him. Now his computer software does that.

Darcy Pohland: Getting the Story

Darcy Pohland was an American journalist. Born in 1961, she grew up in Minnesota. In high school, she was active in music, theater, and marching band. She began college at George Washington University in Washington, DC. When she was 22, she broke her neck in a diving accident. She was paralyzed from the chest down. She spent five months in rehabilitation. Then she continued her studies at the University of Minnesota in Minneapolis.

At the time of her accident, Pohland was an intern at the Washington, DC, office of WCCO. This is a Minneapolis TV station. After finishing college, she was hired at WCCO. First, she was a dispatcher. Then she was an assignment desk editor and a planning editor. In 1994, Pohland became an on-air reporter. She went out in her wheelchair and reported the news. She once broke her wheelchair when she rushed off a curb instead of using the ramp. She wanted to be the first to get an interview.

Pohland's father was a track star at the University of Minnesota in the 1940s. He used to take her to football games. Pohland kept going to games for the rest of her

life. She loved reporting on sports. After her unexpected death in 2010, coworkers remembered her for being a tough reporter and a beautiful writer. She was good at getting people to trust her and tell their stories.

THINK ABOUT IT

Pohland used a special device to type. How have other recent developments in technology made life better for people with disabilities? Try to find two or three examples.

20
Number of years Darcy Pohland worked for WCCO-TV

- Pohland died in her sleep at age 48.
- She was known for her persistence and energy.
- Pohland used assistive devices to type.

Jason Benetti: Hitting a Home Run

at that. He went on to a job with the high school radio station.

Benetti earned a journalism degree from Syracuse University in New York. He earned a law degree from Wake Forest University in North Carolina. He worked as a sports announcer for college and minor leagues. In 2016, the Chicago White Sox needed an announcer. Benetti

Jason Benetti is an American sportscaster. Born 10 weeks early in 1983, he has cerebral palsy (CP). This affects his coordination, movement, and balance. As a child, Benetti had surgery on his eye, heel cord, and hamstring. In high school, he played tuba. When he was too unstable to march with the band, the director asked him to be the announcer. Benetti was good

32

Jason Benetti's age when he called his first nationally televised Major League Baseball game

- Benetti joined the sports brand ESPN in 2011.
- At ESPN, he called college football, baseball and lacrosse telecasts.
- He also called high school football and Little League baseball telecasts.

Benetti preparing for a sports cast of the Syracuse Chiefs in 2013.

had written an essay in elementary school. The topic was "I wonder what I'll be in 20 years." Way back then, he wrote, "I would like to be the White Sox sportscaster." Brooks Boyer, a White Sox vice president, heard that Benetti was one of the best. In January 2016, Benetti got the job.

In 2018, the Cerebral Palsy Foundation (CPF) launched a video campaign called "Awkward Moments with Jason Benetti." Benetti is the voice of a cartoon character based on him. The series shows the humor in awkward social situations. In one video, Benetti is walking in a wobbly way. A woman stares at him. When he looks at her, she quickly looks away. He calls this "The Disability Lookaway." Then he explains how the situation could be less weird for everyone.

AWKWARD MOMENTS
EPISODE 2: THE DISABILITY LOOKAWAY
WITH JASON BENETTI

Ade Adepitan: Paralympian and TV Presenter

Ade Adepitan in 2012.

the United Kingdom. He learned to walk using leg braces.

Adepitan loved sports and dreamed of playing football. When he was 14, he started training for wheelchair basketball. In 2002, he was one of three wheelchair basketball players seen in station identification breaks on BBC TV. In 2005, he won gold at the Paralympics. He completed his first London marathon in 2007.

Ade Adepitan is a TV presenter for the BBC. He was born in Nigeria in 1973. At 15 months, he got polio. The virus caused his left leg to be paralyzed. He has partial use of his right leg. When Adepitan was three, his family moved to

Adepitan went on to host a variety of TV shows. In 2012, he was a TV presenter for the London Paralympics. He co-presented the BBC's *Children in Need* fundraiser series. In 2019, he became the star of a new travel series for BBC. It is called *Africa with Ade Adepitan.*

2005

Year when Ade Adepitan was made a Member of the Most Excellent Order of the British Empire (MBE)

- Adepitan supports the United Kingdom's WheelPower Charity.
- He is an ambassador for Right to Play. This global organization helps children rise above adversity using play.
- He is a celebrity supporter of Sportaid, a group that helps fund athletes.

POLIO

Polio is a highly contagious disease caused by a virus. It destroys the nervous system and causes paralysis. A vaccine was developed in the early 1950s. In the United States, the vaccine ended the disease. In undeveloped countries, children who do not get the vaccine still get polio. The World Health Organization (WHO) works to bring the polio vaccine to children around the world.

8

Jhamak Ghimire: Nepal's Hellen Keller

Jhamak Ghimire is a Nepali writer. Born in the village of Kachide in 1980, she has cerebral palsy (CP). She can't walk or use her hands. She can hear, but she can't speak. In her village, children with disabilities were shunned. They weren't sent to school. Ghimire's grandmother, who cared for her, died when Ghimire was five.

Ghimire had five younger siblings. She watched her father teach her sisters to write. Ghimire wanted to go to school. She used her toes to write in the mud. By watching her sister study, she mastered the alphabet. In time, Ghimire taught herself to read and write. She holds a pen between the toes of her left foot. She began writing poems and articles. The *Kantipur Daily*, her local newspaper, began to print her work.

She got a job writing a column for the *Kantipur Daily*. In 2010, her autobiography was published. It is called *Is Life a Thorn or a Flower?* Ghimire has since published 10 more books. They include poetry, essays, and short stories. The Government of Nepal gives her a monthly salary to live on. Her family now helps take care of her.

Jhamak Ghimire received an honorary degree from Mid-western University in 2016.

HUMAN RIGHTS

The United Nations (UN) is a worldwide organization that works to keep peace between nations and help solve problems for people in need. According to the UN, all human beings have the right to life, liberty, freedom, and the right to work and education. But children with disabilities in Nepal are often denied education. In 2016, 30.6 percent of these children were not sent to school.

3
Functional toes on Jhamak Ghimire's left foot

- Ghimire is called Nepal's Hellen Keller.
- In 2011, her book *Is Life a Thorn or a Flower?* won an important literary award in Nepal.
- The book has been translated into English as *A Flower in the Midst of Thorns.*

Lucy Martin: Weather Presenter and Role Model

Lucy Martin is a British weather presenter. She was born without her right forearm and hand in 1992. As a child, she rode a bike, swam,

and was active in music, dance, and drama. Her family belonged to a group called Reach. There Martin met other children with upper limb differences. She was fitted with prosthetic arms and hands as a child. She never liked wearing them. She found them heavy and unnecessary.

Martin was always interested in weather. She studied geography at Durham University. In 2015, she applied to a workshop offered by the BBC. It was for people with disabilities who wanted to become presenters. She got coaching on storytelling and using her voice. Martin did well and was chosen to train as a presenter. After four months of practice, she did weather reports on the radio. Next, she prerecorded her TV reports. Then she moved on to live reports. She became a full-time BBC weather presenter.

Martin chooses not to wear a prosthetic arm. Her disability is visible to TV viewers. She has gotten positive feedback. Families with children who have disabilities see her as a role model. Many have sent her messages to thank her. Martin

Lucy Martin reports on the weather in the UK.

	Sat	Sun	Mon	Tue	Wed
23	20	21	22	21	

Sat	Sun	Mon	Tue	Wed
11	9	8	8	9

1000s
Number of applicants for the BBC's training program in 2015

- Lucy Martin was one of only 10 people chosen for the program.
- She studied meteorology as part of her geology degree.
- In 2017, her viewers nominated her for an Icon Award. This recognizes people who champion diversity.

raises awareness for people with disabilities. She hopes to be known first as a good weather presenter and second as a person with a disability.

THINK ABOUT IT

Lucy Martin's parents joined a group where Lucy could meet children with similar disabilities. Why was this helpful?

Anderson Cooper: Following His Passion

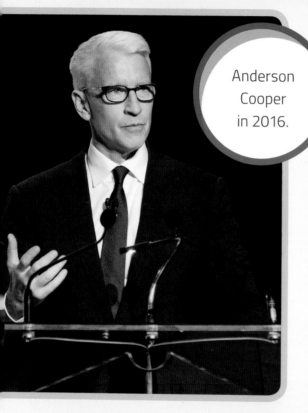

Anderson Cooper in 2016.

Cooper has a mild form of dyslexia. He sees some letters backward. A special reading teacher helped him find books with subjects that interested him. He mastered reading.

Cooper never went to journalism school. He went to a private high school in New York. Then he traveled in Africa before going to Yale University. He earned a degree in political science and international relations. He could have gone into the foreign service. But because of family tragedies, he wanted to know more about why some people survive and others don't. He decided to be a war reporter.

In the years that followed, Cooper traveled to more than 40 countries. Early on, he didn't have a job with a news organization. So he made his own press passes. He covered most of the major news events in the world, often reporting from

Anderson Cooper is a journalist and TV news host. He was born in New York City in 1967. His mother is fashion designer Gloria Vanderbilt. His father was a writer and actor. Cooper appeared in magazines and on TV as a child. He modeled clothes as a preteen.

Cooper moderated the Democratic presidential primary debate in 2016.

the scene. In 2003, Cooper became anchor of *Anderson Cooper 360°* on CNN. In this role, he covers global news.

360 DEGREES

Why does Anderson Cooper use 360° in the name of his news show? When a person turns all the way around in a circle, it's a 360-degree turn. Cooper wants to cover an issue from all sides and all points of view. He is known for his in-depth coverage.

8

Emmy awards Anderson Cooper has won for his reporting

- Cooper was one of the youngest reporters to start at ABC.
- In 2018, he won the Walter Cronkite Award for Excellence in Journalism.
- He is also a contributor to the CBS news show *60 Minutes*.

Wendy Lu: Activist Journalist

Wendy Lu in 2019.

Wendy Lu is an American writer. She was born in 1993. Her parents are from China. She grew up in Boston and North Carolina. Lu has vocal cord paralysis. She breathes through a trach tube (trake toob). This is a small metal or plastic tube worn through a hole in her windpipe. As a child, Lu needed a home care nurse. Today, she lives on her own.

Lu studied journalism at the University of North Carolina. She earned a master's degree from Columbia University in New York. She writes articles for the *New York Times, Teen Vogue,* and *Bustle.* She speaks at schools and conferences. Her focus is on health and social issues. She also writes about gender, politics, disability. She covers lifestyle and culture. In 2018, Lu became a video producer for the *Huffington Post* website.

Lu wants people to change how they write about disabilities. She has tips on how to do this. For example, don't identify someone by their disability. Instead of "the disabled man, John Smith," write "John Smith, reporter." Avoid language that makes readers feel sorry for people with disabilities. Write "Smith has cerebral palsy," not "Smith suffers from cerebral palsy." And stop writing clichéd stories about overcoming disabilities. Write about issues, like police treatment and medical care for people with disabilities.

JOURNALISM

Journalists find, write, and report news. Some write for newspapers and magazines. Some are on the radio and TV. Some share their reporting on the internet, blogs, and podcasts. The goal of journalists is to give people information they need. This helps them make good decisions about their lives, communities, societies, and governments.

19
Percent of the US population with disabilities

- People with disabilities are the largest minority group in the nation.
- Lu champions rights for people with disabilities.
- She calls for newsrooms to hire more people with disabilities.

everyday feminism

Disabled People Don't Need To Be "Fixed" — We Need A Cure For Ableism

May 21, 2018 by Wendy Lu

Columbia Journalism Review.

What journalists can do better to cover the disability beat

By Wendy Lu

Steve Brown: Living His Dream

Steve Brown is a British TV show host. He was born in England in 1981. In elementary school, he played football, cricket, and cross-country. He also loved exploring the wildlife around his home. He watched TV shows about nature and wildlife. He dreamed of one day hosting such a program.

When Brown was 23, he was working in Europe for a tour company. He fell from a first-floor balcony and broke his neck. Brown was paralyzed from the chest down. He spent three weeks in a hospital. Then he was flown to England for rehabilitation. While learning to use a wheelchair, Brown tried archery and table tennis. When he was taken to a wheelchair rugby game, he was inspired.

Brown began training to play the game. In 2006, he competed for the first time. He was on London's team. They won the National Championships. Brown went on to captain Britain's championship team at the Paralympics twice.

Before his accident, Brown had studied film and editing. He was hoping to work on a wildlife TV show. Because of his success playing

Brown (right) playing wheelchair rugby in 2012.

15

Steve Brown's age when a school advisor told him to give up his dream of being a wildlife presenter

- That was before Brown had the accident that left him paralyzed.
- In 2018, Brown won an award from the Royal Television Society for his work on *Countryfile*.
- He works as an athlete mentor for the Youth Sport Trust, a children's national charity. He raises awareness of disability sports and helps young people take part.

wheelchair rugby, he was interviewed by the media. This led to invitations to appear on BBC shows. He worked as a presenter on *Springwatch*, a program about nature and wildlife. In 2017, he became a presenter for the primetime BBC nature show *Countryfile*.

Learn More:
Facts and Figures

- Over a billion people, or 15 percent of the world's population, have a disability.

- Lower-income countries have a higher rate of disability than higher-income countries.

- In the United States, about 74.6 million people have some kind of physical disability.

- African-Americans and Native Americans have the highest rate of disabilities among racial minorities: 24.3 percent for each group.

- In 2013, 17.6 percent of people with a physical disability living in the United States had jobs.

- The most common disability in older adults is mobility, or not being able to walk.

- The most common disability of younger adults is cognitive, or brain-related.

- In 2014, nine percent of American children from ages 13–18 had ADHD.

- In 2014, one in 68 kids had autism.

- Cerebral palsy affects more than 10,000 infants every year.

- One in every 691 children has Down syndrome.

- Students with disabilities are less likely to participate in after-school activities. This leads to less social and leadership skill practice.

- Assistive technology is necessary for more than one-third of people with disabilities to live on their own.

Glossary

anchor
A person who presents the news on TV.

article
A report or essay in the news.

cliché
A phrase or way of writing that is used too often and is not original.

column
A report that appears on a regular basis in the news.

commentator
An expert who gives insight into the news.

conservative
In politics, someone who believes that government should be limited and people should have the freedom to pursue their own goals.

discriminate
To treat unfairly on the basis of a difference such as a disability.

global
Worldwide.

liberal
In politics, someone who believes that government should act to achieve equal opportunity and equality for all.

media
Different ways to deliver news, such as radio, TV, the internet, or newspapers.

rehabilitate
To restore to health.

shun
To ignore and avoid.

Read More

Dell, Pamela. *Understanding the News.* Mankato, MN: Capstone Press, 2019.

Hunt, Jilly. *Human Rights for All.* Mankato, MN: Capstone Press, 2018.

Mahoney, Ellen. *Nellie Bly and Investigative Journalism for Kids: Mighty Muckrakers from the Golden Age to Today.* Chicago,IL: Chicago Review Press, 2015.

Visit 12StoryLibrary.com

Scan the code or use your school's login at **12StoryLibrary.com** for recent updates about this topic and a full digital version of this book. Enjoy free access to:

- Digital ebook
- Breaking news updates
- Live content feeds
- Videos, interactive maps, and graphics
- Additional web resources

Note to educators: Visit 12StoryLibrary.com/register to sign up for free premium website access. Enjoy live content plus a full digital version of every 12-Story Library book you own for every student at your school.

Index

Adepitan, Ade, 16-17
ambassador, 17

Benetti, Jason, 14-15
Brown, Steve, 26-27

commentator, 8-9
Cooper, Anderson, 22-23

discrimination, 11

Ghimire, Jhamak, 18-19

human rights, 19, 25

investigative reporter,
4-5

Kovaleski, Serge, 4-5
Krauthammer, Charles,
8-9

Lu, Wendy, 24-25

Martin, Lucy, 20-21

O'Donoghue, Gary, 10-
11

Pohland, Darcy, 12-13
Pulitzer Prize, 5, 9, 10

raising awareness, 21,
27

reporter, 6-7, 10-11,
12-13

Searing, Laura Redden,
6-7
sportscaster, 14-15

TV news host, 22-23
TV show host, 16-17,
26-27

weather presenter, 20-
21
writer, 18-19, 24-25

About the Author

Marne Ventura is the author of over 100 books for children. A former elementary school teacher, she holds a master's degree in education from the University of California. Marne and her husband live on the central coast of California.

READ MORE FROM 12-STORY LIBRARY

Every 12-Story Library Book is available in many fomats. For more information, visit **12StoryLibrary.com**